BAD TASTE

Self-Care and Financial Planning
When You Have
BAD TASTE in Men

Mary Crocker Cook, PH.D., D.Min., LMFT, LAADC
Illustrated by Adrienne Pinkman

Bad Taste
Self-care and Financial Planning When You Have Bad Taste in Men

Copyright © 2024 Mary Crocker Cook

ISBN: 978-1-61170-328-3

All rights reserved. No part of this publication may be reproduced, stored in a retrieval system or transmitted in any form or by any means, electronic, mechanical, photocopies, recording or otherwise, without the prior written consent of the publisher, except in the case of brief quotations embodied in critical reviews.

Published by:

www.RobertsonPublishing.com

Printed in the USA and UK on acid-free paper.

*This small book was written for
all the marvelous women, and the friends who love them,
on their imperfect journey towards more serenity.*
We got this.

Contents

Introduction 1

He's Married 5

He's an Addict/Alcoholic 10

He Has Untreated Mental Illness 16

He's a Criminal 20

He Has a Personality Disorder 25

He Hates to Work 30

He Is a User 33

He Comes and Goes 38

He Is Emotionally Immature 42

He's a Cheater 47

Conclusion 53

Quizzes to Consider if You
are on a Journey to Shift Your Patterns 55
    What Is My Attachment Style? 56
    Responses to Stressful Experiences Scale 61

Contact Information 63

Introduction

Despite years of therapy and personal long-term recovery, everyone who loves me will tell you I have often displayed the worst taste in men. Why the focus only on men? I am writing from a cis-female life experience vantage point, and so cannot speak with authority about the experiences of others. I KNOW the types I am identifying are found across gender and sexual worlds, and I encourage you, as we say in recovery, to *"take what you like and leave the rest."* What I can say with authority is that I personally chose some version of unavailable or unreliable repeatedly! As a therapist over the last 40 years, I have watched other smart, funny, responsible, loving women choose mates unwisely as well. There are those of us who simply should not be allowed to choose for ourselves!

Let's define our terms. When I say, "Bad Taste," I mean that the more my eyes sparkled, the more everyone who loves me could feel their gut drop. I just never seemed to choose in my own best interest.

Here are some examples I have seen or experienced:

- The guy that lets you know he is newly divorced and has supervised visitation with his daughter because of his anger management problems.
- The guy who tells you, because he has no filter, that he would like to sleep with your best friend.
- The guy who recently left his wife for another woman online, and then dumped her when he met her because she was fat.
- The guy with no papers has already been deported once.
- The guy who is married but says to you when you try to break it off, "We'll work something out."
- The guy that orders five Jack Daniels in one hour on your first date.
- The guy that hates his mother and goes on and on about what a bitch his ex is.
- He's your brother-in-law, father-in-law, husband's best friend, teacher, or therapist.

God love us, we can't seem to help ourselves. Our heart "wants what it wants."

Maybe you have fallen in love with a man your children clearly hate because he is a control freak. One weekend while they are with their dad, you and your new love impulsively fly to Vegas and get married. When the children come back, he is moving in, and you feel like the children are overreacting when they want to live with their dad—after all, "They can't tell me who to marry!"

Or you have married your sister's ex-husband and are planning to have him join the family for Thanksgiving dinner. You figure, THEY need to be more supportive and get over it. Her marriage was over five years ago!

You have just met a man who lights you up like a Christmas tree. He is looking to settle down. In fact, you know he loves commitment because he has already been married five times so is not afraid to say, "I do." This time, he is sure YOU are the one he has been waiting for all these years.

A woman gets a referral for a handyman for home improvements. He arrives, two months abstinent from crack, and within a week she moves him into her house to make the remodel more "convenient." SHE is going to be his path to ongoing recovery.

You are dating a man who you suddenly discover has married someone else when you thought you were engaged! When confronted, he admits he married her, but it was only for "immigration" or "financial" reasons, so it doesn't really count. He really loves you. You spend the next five years fighting over his "promise" to file divorce papers.

It reminds me of a makeover show I watched several years ago where someone's friends would write into the show and beg them to do a wardrobe intervention with their friend because she/he was a disaster.

Honey, if you are honest with yourself, your friends have already plotted YOUR intervention. In the meantime, I want to do what we call in the recovery business, "harm reduction," and help you protect yourself in the middle of your bad decision-making in men.

Here's a note on why these choices keep happening:

Someone can be incredibly accomplished and stable in most areas of their lives, yet have a giant hole in their relationship skills.

It is tempting to say to yourself, "What was I thinking?" and "Why don't I remember what happened last time?" or "He's such a jerk; why didn't I see it?" I have certainly thought these things at times when sitting on the other side of a fabulous woman who is sharing her excitement over her latest hopeless choice.

However, our intellect is not doing the choosing. Most of my work, particularly with people with a history of being invisible, traumatized, or abandoned, is to help them connect their head and their heart. We have a working model of how relationships unfold that we replay over and over again. It's as though when the possibility of attachment happens, it surprises us, and our judgment goes out the window. When I say, "God love us—we can't help ourselves," I mean it.

When I think about my own impulse to "Say yes to the dress" with someone unlikely, it rarely is from my head. In fact, my head says, "This is highly unlikely; don't get your hopes up," and my heart (my emotionally abandoned inner child) says, "Yes, but MAYBE."

When I was making a passionate case about why he may LOOK like he is a terrible choice, but here's why he's different, know that my inner child was speaking. This is what gives me patience and compassion both for myself and others. Is it possible to change this? YES IT IS. In fact, if you go to www.marycrockercookbooks.com you will find books addressing this attachment interruption and healing process. **However, that is not the purpose of this little book**. Our purpose here is to address how to stay as stable as possible either in the middle of your **BAD TASTE** choices while you are working on yourself or if you have already surrendered to your questionable selections. To keep things from being TOO dark, I will offer some thoughts about healing along the way, because if you are reading this, you ARE already healing. You are paying attention to what you can change, which is yourself, instead of understanding and explaining *him*, which is something you cannot change. Our power lies in our own agency.

I was laughing about my unwise selection history with my home girl when I mentioned that someone should write a book about how to take care of ourselves for women like me, and she remarked, "Why not you?" I thought, "Why not me?" After all, I am a subject matter expert, and despite my history of **BAD TASTE in men,** I have been successful in other areas of my life. In fact, when you purchase this book, know that we have created a downloadable PDF, *"Support for Friends of Women with BAD TASTE in Men,"* so people who care about you can manage their role in loving you through your inevitable disappointments.

Bad Taste

What follows is the result of hard-won lessons in my life as well as others I have seen over the years. There is a way to maintain some sanity and financial stability despite our broken "picker." I promise: You too can survive your incredibly **BAD TASTE** in men as you move forward.

Chapter One:

He's Married

It would seem obvious that this would be a "no-hoper" from the gate, and 95% of the time it ends in tears. However, for women like me, hope springs eternal! We "know" intellectually we should run when he says:

1. We haven't been sexual for years
2. We are only together for the sake of the children
3. The marriage has been dead for years
4. We have nothing in common except the children
5. Our religions don't allow divorce
6. We have to live together in separate rooms because we can't afford a divorce
7. Add your own…

Somehow, we tell ourselves, "But I'll be the exception," or "I'll wait until the kids graduate and THEN we can be together," or [fill in the blank].

Maybe he's the married co-worker who has the same work style and sense of humor. You never INTENDED for the small flirtations to grow, and then one afternoon you are caught off guard by an unexpected kiss. You are confused, excited, and vaguely guilty. What should you do? Well, WE will most likely pretend it is not that big a deal and let the chips fall where they may! After all, he's married, and we aren't. Isn't it up to him to rein it in?

Maybe you have been traveling with another couple for years; they are always part of the planning! You spend holidays together, birthdays together, celebrate children together. Then one day while cleaning up after yet another holiday gathering, your husband's friend tells you he can no longer lie to himself anymore, and he MUST tell you how much he thinks about you, dreams about you … feels overwhelmed by you. What should you do? Well, WE might panic a little at first, but then we might begin to start ruminating on all the time we have spent with him, and recognize we have feelings too. This never ends well.

One possible solution is to create other ways to "be together" like becoming business partners (I lost $30,000 this way) or join an adult sports team, or even become "coaches" for Little League in order to have a connection. We offer to help them build their company, give them support and counsel about their bad marriage or troubled children. We arrange our schedule to accommodate their lives because they are already under enough stress, and we don't want to be one more stressor.

We remain steadfast in our excuse-making and twisted logic about how we really are a "couple" despite their obvious unavailability. We go to every funeral, wedding, special event alone because they can't attend. We loudly proclaim, "I understand" as though we don't mind.

I am not here to judge this poor choice—God knows I have been there and suffered the consequences in every way imaginable. I have sat across from men and women who wept as the reality of their decision-making increasingly encroached on their lives, and they could no longer pretend it was "fine."

Here is what I have learned:

Don't lie to yourself about the situation. He is not available, and likely you are not his first "extra" relationship. I remember a long time ago working with a wonderful woman who fell for her married co-worker, and as she described what sounded like increased flirtation in her relationship with him, I remember pointing out to her that it sounded like they were preparing to "move to the next level," which would be physical. I didn't judge her, but instead laid out the reality of his lack of availability, so she could make the decision to proceed or not with her eyes wide open.

Sure enough, within a few weeks the first stolen kisses began, and it was on. No, he did not leave his wife. Yes, she was hurt when he took a job elsewhere (mostly to get away from her), but she was not a "victim." She was a sad volunteer, but she moved through her sadness a little more quickly because we were able to look at HER availability for relationships, which was the real issue.

If you DO walk away with him, know that you have chosen a cheater (see the last section), and so it will most likely happen to you, too. Your foundation for trust will be rocky from the start.

Creating a separate world where you can be together, like starting a business or becoming soccer "coaches," will not work because **his family will STILL come first**, and then you will be stuck running the business or the team at all the inconvenient and holiday times because he has to be there "for the children." You will have to take care of things while he vacations with his family, and you will have to look at family photos in his office if you are his co-worker. GIIRRRRLLLLL, I can promise you that carrying the business or shared obligations while he is on a family outing will create more resentment than you can possibly imagine.

If you DO make the mistake, like I did, of creating a business, double check that your name is on it. I did not do this, and when it went south, I had to start all over. He put his wife's name on it! It was shocking as I sat in a lawyer's office trying to get my $30,000 dollars back and getting hit with this news.

Do not blend your money with his in a business or loan him money for his new venture. I know you are pretending that it is like having a joint account, like a couple, but it's not.

If you give him gifts, he has to keep them at the office or hidden in his car and cannot take them home. So you will look at the gifts and pretend that the office is "your space" with him. It is not. When I got dumped by my guy for another bimbo (because honestly, I was acting like one), when he left me AND his wife, he boxed up everything I ever gave him and dumped it in my driveway. This was easy for him, because IT WAS ALL IN HIS OFFICE!

Save the money you want to spend on gifts and business ventures in your own savings account, so that when you have to end the relationship, you have the money to start over in a new location if you need to.

If he gives you gifts, ask for jewelry. Why? You can sell it when it goes south and make back some of the money you lost on him. You need to plan for the ending, even if you are holding out hope. You can wear the jewelry when you are together to pretend it means you are in a relationship. But think of it as a savings account. In fact, after most of my disaster relationships, I bought myself a diamond. Unfortunately, I have a large collection.

Hold onto your friendships, even if your friends disapprove, because you will need their support at some point. It may mean you need to suffer a few "I told you so's," but they love you and will agree with you that you may be an idiot, but he is REALLY a bastard. You will need this during the anger part of a break-up. In fact, they can even point out horrible incidents you have deliberately forgotten in order to shore up your commitment to never make this mistake again. **If they ever point out that the friendship has become imbalanced because you are taking up all the oxygen with your latest "man drama," hear them and back up.** Honestly, it will do you good to hear about someone else OTHER than you, and you really do love them.

I never had the bad taste to fall in love with a married man again but had so many other versions that I needed my friends! *Make sure to direct your friends to the PDF I mentioned in the beginning!*

If you try to integrate him into your family gatherings, even though he is married to someone else, be prepared for a mixed response. Regardless of how sympathetic his "tale" is ("my wife is permanently disabled, and we can never have a 'full' marriage"), not everyone in your family is going to be able to embrace your decision. They may even request that you not bring him to family gatherings or not tell "grandma" because she will "lose her shit" if she finds out. **It is a lot to ask your family members to enter the "secret" world you have created for yourself, so think long and hard about asking them to join you there for someone who will most likely not be permanent.** Including him in your family doesn't make him any less married.

Make sure you still have parts in your world that do not include him. For example, your gym, your hobbies, your recovery meetings—you need spaces you can go that do not remind you of your time with him. In fact, this leads me to my next point . . .

DO NOT BRING HIM TO YOUR HOUSE. If at all possible, when you "hook up," do it at the office, the car, in a hotel, even his house, if you must. The last thing you need is a physical reminder of your time with him when it goes south. Go on vacation with him, etc. Do your best NOT to have your living space, and your cats, imprinted with him.

Please do not do as one woman I know did and buy her home strategically near his so that he could come spend time with her there and "play house." She did this for 20 years waiting for his children to leave the home so he "could" leave. I am sure she adored him, but two decades is a long time.

Again, WHY are we in, or staying in, this situation? We could be afraid of commitment ourselves; we could have grown up learning to "settle" because there was not enough love to go around; or we may have a fantasy that if he chooses us instead of her it means we are REALLY loved. *I would encourage you to spend time with people who can fully focus on you, think about you when they are away from you, and offer unstructured and unconditional love* so that you will have a felt memory of being truly loved when it ends. *No matter how it ends, try to remember that the universe is throwing you a lifeline—you are being pulled out of a sinkhole*, *and you get a chance to regroup and start again.*

Chapter Two

He's an Addict/Alcoholic

I have a great deal of experience here both personally and as an addiction specialist. When I am referring to Addict/Alcoholic, I am including sex addition, gambling, substance use, food, gaming, marijuana—simply put, people who use substances and activities to trigger a dopamine hit that delivers a temporary high and changes the way they feel. The end result is that the person is not available, consistently, for a full relationship.

A relationship with an active addict is an emotional rollercoaster, but ultimately very lonely. You will spend a lot of time waiting, hoping, clock-watching, being pissed off about the constant lying, and checking your phone and bank account.

If you are lucky, they will seek treatment, and you will walk with them through rehab and attend family meetings where you can learn how you have been affected by their addiction. Sadly, for many of us, our first addiction experience was in our childhood, so we have some mad skills for making a relationship work in these circumstances. God knows, because they could potentially die, we don't quit on the people we love easily. However, if we aren't careful, we will be pulled in trying to help them off the cliff only to go over it with them. There are lots of books written for families and loved ones of addicts and alcoholics, and there are several ways to seek effective intervention. I am going to address this from a self-protective angle.

A relationship with someone committed to addictive behavior with no plan or desire to stop means this: They WILL be drinking or using, and it will be part of the relationship.

Occasionally, the person will flat out admit that they will die before stopping their addictive behavior, so the choice will be clear. Most of the time, though, they will say they will quit when they are ready and leave out some hope we can cling to. What I am going to say may be hard to hear, but I have learned this personally and professionally.

When you love someone who will not stop, there is no happy ending. Here is the short version:

I remember when I loved a man who was a few years sober, and we had not seen each other for a year because I had left the relationship when he became verbally abusive. Out of the blue, he called me, drunk, and begged me to come and see him. I drove over, and he was barely able to walk, had peed on his couch, and when I put him to bed, got up and peed in the closet. I had to hold him up to shower, and there was no food or toilet paper in the house.

I came by the next day with food and supplies, and he had cuts all over his face because he had walked to the liquor store and fallen in front of his house on his face. As I put his food away, I saw him fall backwards in his chair and hit his head again on the electric heater. It was horrifying.

He was unwilling to go to detox. I knew from working in treatment that at his level of drinking, at some point he would be unable to walk. So I left and told him to call me when that happened. In between, he would call and want to have long rambling drunkalogues that I would cut short. Finally, the day came when he was not answering the phone, and I went over and found him having soiled his pants on the couch and unable to walk. At this point, I called the ambulance, who took him to the hospital and checked him in blowing a BAL of 4.5. He was delusional and in intensive care detox for two weeks.

He was hardy and did not die. He was eventually discharged to a sober living home. Sober for a month or two, he then disappeared. Just . . . vanished. I assumed he was dead, honestly. He wasn't; he eventually popped up and called me from a hospital. I had him at my house for three days until there was an opening and checked him into a sober living center, and that was it. After he left, I found bottles hidden all over my house. He had stolen all the quarters I had set aside for the coin-operated laundry in my complex. So even then, he was still sneaking out and buying booze. The kicker? He peed on *my* couch, too!

Here is what I have learned:

Addiction can lead to significant legal and medical bills. If the person you love is not going to stop using their substance, then **you need to create a barrier between you financially.** You may even need to divorce him, even if you stay with him, to protect yourself from the debt incurred by their substance use. DUIs and liver failure are scary—and very expensive.

If he has a DUI, he will need to install a breathalyzer in his car for about 150.00 and pay a monthly lease of about 100.00. He may need an ankle bracelet which will run about 20.00 a day to avoid incarceration.

Private substance use disorder treatment is expensive IF he agrees to go. A 30-day stay, even WITH good insurance will have a several thousand-dollar co-pay. Out of pocket, you will be looking at between $20,000 to $80,000 for the month, depending on how swanky a place you choose. You can also go through the county if you do not have insurance, and there will be a waiting list, so he may have a delay before entering, which will give him time to change his mind. Outpatient treatment is more affordable but still about $3,000 a month, and if he needs a sober living home for transition, this will run about $800 a month.

Make sure you are on the lease if you are renting, so you will not have your housing interrupted by his absence. Make sure you can afford it without his income down the road because, unfortunately, substance use disorder is a relapsing disease. The last thing you need is to have to look for housing in your grief over his absence. You need to make sure that you:

- Have an income yourself, no matter how small.
- Have at least one credit card in your name that you use and pay off monthly to create credit in your name. The better your credit score, the more options you have.
- Set money aside in a separate account in case you need to take care of yourself and your kids quickly. If possible, have your paycheck direct-deposited to your personal account, and then add money to a joint household account for shared expenses.

To love someone who will not stay or get sober means they have a terminal illness; you have to accept the anxiety of this. I know it sounds grim, and addiction is. The end point for many addicts is death, prison, disappearing. **It means you must love them when they are occasionally available**, KNOWING it is temporary, and they will be unavailable again.

This is going to sound silly, but I still have a memory of my friend and I sharing a wonderful afternoon when he was moderately drunk. We were both lying on the floor because walking was challenging to him and were laughing and singing together. We were listening to music, and even all these years later, I smile at that memory. I knew he was ill but decided to just enter the moment with him. I am so glad I did.

I have another friend, a guy I briefly dated, who I quickly discovered was a serious alcoholic, and I have a similar memory of a New Year's Eve when he came by, and we laughed and fooled around when he was moderately drunk. He then went out and drank so heavily, he fell headfirst off a ladder. He disappeared soon after. He was a sweet guy and completely committed to alcoholism.

If you are married to a committed addict, and you have a chance to share a meal or a family event with him when he is only moderately impaired, you may want to take advantage of it. Just make sure he isn't driving you or the kids, so you can leave if you need to. The person you loved still occasionally peeks out, and you know what times of day are better than others. There may come a time when his behavior when loaded or impaired is so noxious or even dangerous you will no longer be able to have these moments. So, seize them when you can.

If you are married, especially with children, you MUST have a life insurance policy that is current and substantial. Do this even though it makes you more likely to appear on Dateline! You need your medical plan to be current. If you are not married but living together and he is willing to admit he will never stop, he needs **to create a will so you can avoid probate when he passes.** He may not be able to get a life insurance plan if he is too ill, but he can create a will and **put you on his bank account so you can pay bills as well as his funeral and medical debt.** Better yet, get everything, including the cell carrier and the PG&E in your name.

If he routinely drinks and drives, you may consider NOT having your name on the pink slip if he tends to get in wrecks and let his license, insurance and tags lapse. If he is arrested while drinking, the car will be sent to impound, and you have a short window to pay to get it back, which is another reason you will need an extra $1,500 put aside. If possible, have a car that he doesn't drive in your name so you can keep the tags and insurance up to date. **If you share the car, then you will have to take the responsibility to make sure everything is current**. If you can afford it, get the best coverage you can. You might need it.

The same caveat goes for taxes. If you are married, you are liable for the tax debt, and people who are committed to using substances are not always on top of the paperwork. **You will have to make sure your taxes are filed and property taxes are paid if you own your own home.** Do not let yourself get surprised by a huge tax bill when the IRS seizes your account!

If your man uses drug paraphernalia like needles, pipes, or spoons, etc. and has no plans to stop using, negotiate a safe place for drug use if you have children. Maybe it's a specific bathroom or somewhere in the garage where he keeps his drugs and paraphernalia inaccessible from the children. Honestly, it is better that you do not see him using; it is hard to watch. It is hard enough to see him under the influence. If it's porn, he needs a laptop separate from the family devices. Same thing if it is online betting. **Keep his drug and addiction supply purchases separate from the family finances—he needs a separate financial source, if possible.**

Which reminds me . . . addicts also can sell your possessions if they "need" the money. **So, if you have heirlooms from your grandmother and other valuables, get a safety deposit box, and do not tell him**. You will need to use it from time to time if you want your children to have heirlooms to inherit. Same thing when inheriting money or property. Keep the deeds in the safety deposit box.

I remember a woman called me once to relay the happy news that her active addict boyfriend had proposed with a beautiful diamond ring. She was very much in love with him, and still, in the same conversation with me, mentioned that she asked him if he had stolen the ring! Later on, she found that the answer was "yes," and then he stole her car. Sigh. Let's be candid here: If it even crosses your mind to ask him if the ring is stolen, you are in the BAD TASTE club!

Finally, if your man is a gambler, you need to keep a close eye on any shared savings account, household financing, and credit cards. I once worked with a woman who discovered that her husband spent their entire savings on sports betting when she went to pre-qualify on a home. $400,000 was gone. I had another person who had won the lottery, which was supposed to be for the couple's retirement, and his partner discovered it had all been lost due to online gaming. Not only was there no retirement money, but there was a $100,000 IRS bill!

Again, I am sorry to be so direct, but I have watched too many women NOT protect themselves and then be financially as well as emotionally devastated because they were **afraid to address the reality of the situation.**

The good news is—and there is good news—you DO NOT have to wait for him to get sober to get support and help for yourself. I am a 35-year veteran of the Twelve-Step program Al-Anon myself, which is the Twelve-Step program for friends and family of alcoholics. We learn to take care of ourselves and reduce the impact on our sanity of someone else's drinking. There is also Nar-Anon for families of drug users, Al-A-Teen and Al-A-Tot for children. These programs offer a lifeline to the whole family and take place in-person and online. One of the gifts of COVID was the rapid increase in Zoom meetings all over the world, so help is only a click away.

There are intervention programs like Community Reinforcement and Family Training (CRAFT) when the addict is invited to the healing process, but it is not necessary. You and your family can move forward in recovery regardless of the sobriety of the other person.

Please gather as many tools as you can because the impact of addiction is a marathon and not a sprint!

Chapter Three

He Has Untreated Mental Illness

This is also a very challenging situation, often because men like this pull on our heartstrings, and we feel compelled to help or be their stabilizing force. After all, if we can "love" them enough, they will get better, right?

I am specifically saying **untreated mental illness** here, because when most mental health issues are addressed, they can be managed. There are exceptions, and I will address those in another section. The primary issue is whether he will acknowledge his mental health issue and participate in treatment. It is very hard to live with him when he insists that HE is not the problem.

I am thinking here of things like ADHD, bipolar disorder, thought disorders, anxiety disorders, or major depression. What all of these have in common is mood instability and poor emotional regulation. This means he is more prone to looking for external emotional management like substances or the other people in their household. He can become under-functioning or dramatic when his symptoms flare up, and then the often over-functioning woman in his life picks up the slack and serves as the stabilizer for the household. This comes at great cost to her.

Managing a relationship with someone who has significant mood shifts is both emotionally and financially destabilizing. When he is symptomatic, he may:

- Not be responsive when asked for support or help around the house
- Be a really poor listener and not retain information well
- Not work steadily, or ONLY work and then check out at home
- Display anger, irritability, overreaction, over-control, hyperactive talking, or suck up all the emotional energy in the house. He may be what a friend said his wife called him: "The black cloud."

I ventured into this territory years ago with a smart, well-educated man who would not treat his depression. When he got laid off, I have a searing memory of him in his blue terrycloth bathrobe sitting at his computer when I left for work, and him still in the bathrobe when I came home.

There were long periods of silence, and he was so hard to engage. I did discover that he was engaged one day, though, when I opened the computer, and a naked picture of him popped up, which linked to a dating site. While it was a gut-punch, it gave me hope in a weird way that at least he was capable of something! We did not last long after that. I still cannot stand to look at a blue terrycloth bathrobe!

I am thinking of another fabulous woman I know who married an absolutely charming man who told her he was bipolar, but did NOT tell her that he was not willing to take medication consistently. **Make sure to research his disorder. Know what the symptoms are, so you know what not to take personally.** Untreated manic episodes are hard on the household—he will not sleep very much, will talk a lot, be irritable, unreasonable, make poor spending decisions, be impulsive, and maybe hyper-sexual. In a serious depressive episode, he can become suicidal, sleep 16 hours a day, be cognitively slow, have poor concentration. You will need a plan to manage you and your children when these episodes happen.

If he is struggling with untreated ADHD, learn about it. It is hard not to take his inattention and distractions personally, but they are not personal. You will need to find a way to engage with him that includes eye contact, getting to the point, and a solid reminder system like a large white-board calendar. You need to set aside a space in the house where he can create piles and stack things that has a door you can shut. This allows you to negotiate different uncluttered areas for the rest of the household. **This means investing in an organization system for the home that accommodates his neurodivergent challenges, which will be worth every penny!**

On the upside, men who are neurodivergent tend to not be liars or the type to play games. They might be oblivious to social and emotional cues at times, but they do well with patterns and routines and so can be incredibly reliable. Inflexibility during transitions can be challenging, but preparing for this ahead of time makes this doable. In other words, avoid surprises!

Here is what I have learned:

To stay functioning for yourself, YOU need a support system that is not erratic, recognizes your social cues, and is available. You may need sudden assistance with childcare because he has stopped responding, or his memory is unreliable. You may need a place to stay for a few days while he is manic because he doesn't sleep, or is lost in paranoia, or is verbally aggressive, and you need to sleep in order to keep going to work. In this type of relationship, you may not be able to work remotely if they are home a lot because they can be intrusive.

You need to create a schedule and routine that can function with or without his participation. When he asymptomatic and available, he can be there for you and be a partner, which is why you keep hanging in there. However, under stress or increase in symptoms, he may not have that capability, and, in fact, your workload will increase to manage him.

Untreated mental health issues can also be expensive. You may need to find a way to make home repairs yourself or be able to hire help. You will need Uber to take you places when you need a ride because he may check out. He may have unstable employment. Your own health may suffer due to stress, and you will have your own medical bills, which might include therapy and psychiatric support.

He might have outstanding legal and medical bills acquired during an episode that you will need to manage, so you may need an extra credit card with your name only on it with at least a $5,000 limit.

Okay, I know you are seeing a theme here when I suggest that **you have your own income source.** The point of money is that it gives you OPTIONS. Consider some of the ideas I suggest in a later section—ways to get certified quickly and beginning earning some steady money even if you don't go to work right away.

See his money as a bonus, not primary income, even if he is making A LOT of money. If he makes a lot of money, open your own account and start adding to it. This is because if it goes south, the same mental illness that hijacked the marriage will also hijack the divorce proceedings, and he will be difficult to work with in the separation negotiations if he decides to file. **Divorce or separation is very stressful, so he will be symptomatic.** Plan on it and draw on the money you have set aside if he suddenly cancels the credit cards and withdraws all the money from the bank account. **And for God's sake, do NOT try mediation**. Go straight to an attorney. A person with untreated mental illness that creates this level of instability cannot negotiate in good faith, because the minute they have a mood swing, whatever was agreed upon will be fair game.

The good news is there are agencies like NAMI (National Alliance for the Mentally Ill) that provide invaluable support. They can help you AND the man you love. They have a treasure trove of referral sources, support groups, training courses, and even often have a Peer training program. They can help you navigate the confusing mental health system and connect you with the resources you need.

There is also CHADD (Children and Adults with Attention Deficit Disorder) that can also connect you with ADD coaches, support groups, training, and materials that will give you more confidence to stabilize the family you love. You do not have to figure this out by yourself.

Chapter Four
He's a Criminal

I confess that this one has been a weakness of mine and the subject of hours of therapy. I think it is because I am an over-responsible child of an alcoholic who rarely gives myself permission to be a flake. These men, on the other hand, have all kinds of permission internally to do whatever they feel like. They are NOT overburdened by worry about consequences. (Maybe that's why I cannot watch enough Dateline episodes!)

There are several challenges in a relationship with a man who goes in and out of incarceration **with no plan to change his criminality**. On the one hand, it can be comforting if you are the jealous type, because you always know where he is! On the other hand, phone conversations and weekend visits can only go so far. You are often lonely, and you will be doing your life by yourself most of the time because he isn't available.

Here is what I have learned:

Actively criminal men can be expensive partners in many ways

You might be evicted because their employment may not be steady, and eviction makes it harder to rent another place. You will have to pay more deposit to get a place, and it tears up your credit. **If you are not going to jail yourself, put YOUR name on the lease so you don't have to move every time he goes to jail or skips town,** and your kids won't have to change schools.

When your man gets arrested, he vanishes—his employment is interrupted, and he can no longer participate physically in your life. If you are fortunate, you have the **money to bail him out, which is 10% of the total bail if you use a bail bondsman**. The 10% you pay up front will depend on how serious his crime is and the level of risk the court determines he is to the community. The bond is non-refundable, so you will not get the 10% back. However, if you can quickly get him out, and he can keep working, you can make the money back. This is the best-case scenario. Worst case, he sits in jail, and probably loses his job, while he waits for arraignment and can plead out or go to trial.

Then you must get an attorney. If you do not have money, you can get a public defender assigned and, given the backlog, he will sit in jail for a while. Otherwise, **you need to get a private criminal attorney, and they will want a retainer**. Depending on the seriousness of the charge, it can be thousands of dollars up front. They will take your retainer and put it in "trust" for your case and draw against it to pay for every letter they write, call they have with you, or court appearance. When that money runs out, they will ask for another chunk. This can rack up quickly, so you can't afford to call and write to them every time you have a thought. They are not your support person.

You may need to find a job, a better job, and need help with childcare in your man's absence if he was helping. If you have family and friends who can step in, that is the best case. Otherwise, you need to find the money for the childcare hours he was covering.

I would consider getting trained for fields where you can be certified to work in a year or less, especially through a community college where tuition is low or free, and you may very well qualify for grants.

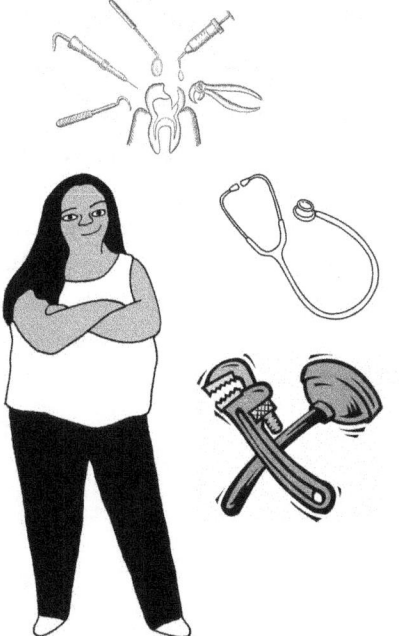

Trades: Electricians, Plumbing, Carpentry, Welding all are paid well, and you can develop a marketable skill that will allow you to do side jobs to earn extra money.

Medical field: Phlebotomist, Radiation Tech, Dental Hygienist, even medical transcribing are in demand and pay well.

Legal: if you love research and writing, and are good with details, you can become a Paralegal within 2 years.

These are ideas—and there are more. The goal is to make sure you can take care of yourself fairly quickly. THEN, you can take classes a few at a time to pursue a degree, if this is a goal for you.

On another note, when your man is arrested in a raid, your property becomes what is called *criminal forfeiture*. They can take your house and possessions if they connect them with your man's crime. You may or may not get them back. **So, again, have a safety deposit box somewhere separate for YOUR valuables,** because once they are seized, they could be sold off in the criminal justice process.

Similar to financial concerns when partnered with an addict, **you need to stay on top of taxes and other financial obligations to keep your housing and life stable.** Criminals often do not see rules or obligations as applying to them, and so disregard them.

People going in and out of jail are frequently behind in their child support payments, and when they do finally go to work, their wages will be garnished. They may have an outstanding bill, and this is a **large argument for NOT MARRYING him**, because when you do, whoever he owes money to can go after you financially as well. The same is true for his outstanding tax bill.

I once advised a client to insist that her recovering alcoholic fiancé's back taxes be resolved BEFORE she walked down the aisle. He did this for her, which I saw as a good sign!

On the other hand, I knew a woman who had met her man shortly before he went to jail, and upon his release she moved him in with her so she could help him pay off his IRS bill and help him pay his back taxes so they could start saving for their own home. I only saw the couple once, because it was clear that he was not going to stay in the relationship now that his obligations had been met. He had told her he was leaving, and I think she hoped I would change his mind. It broke my heart for her. **Being his financial solution does not guarantee a lifelong commitment, honey, I promise.**

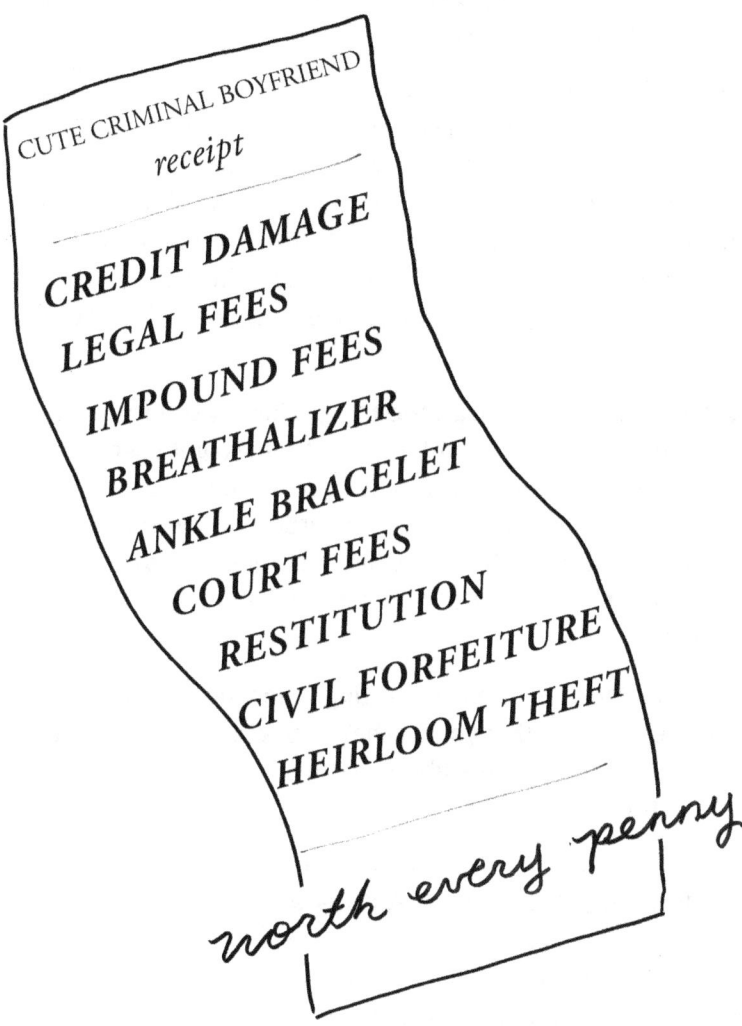

I also sat with a heartbroken man one time who had met the love of his life a week before she was arrested, and he had already bought her an engagement ring. He brought her home when she was released, and when he went to work the next day, she cleaned him out and disappeared. Ultimately, she did him a favor, but his tears were real.

Do NOT have a child with someone facing or serving a life sentence. I am not being silly here; this is something I have seen many times. If you have a child with someone serving 25 years to life you will be a single parent. I know having a child creates a connection between you and gives you the illusion of a family, but the reality is it will be a long-distance relationship and long-distance parenting. It is not romantic, and it is hard on the child.

Depending on where he is serving time, you may need to travel to visit him and bring his child, which means you will stand in line a lot and might even need to get a hotel. You might also spend a lot in gas, and **you will be sending him money so he can buy what he needs in the commissary while he is incarcerated.** If it is a life sentence, this is a very long obligation. However, he will be sending you lots of letters and drawings, so if your love language is writing, he will make your heart happy!

He will also be calling you all the time, which is collect, so that bill can rack up over time. He has nothing BUT time, so get used to hearing the opening announcement in the call requiring you to accept the call and know it can, and very like will be, recorded. Know that he will expect you to answer EVERY TIME he calls, regardless of what you might be doing, which includes the two to three jobs you are working to make ends meet.

Now, if you PREFER single parenting, then he might be the perfect choice. Keep in mind that you will have selected a criminal sperm donor. Depending on your beliefs about nature versus nurture, you need to think this through.

Bottom line: If you want to date a criminal, much like an addict, HAVE YOUR OWN INCOME AND CHECKING ACCOUNT. When he is home, and is working legally or illegally, there will be money there. But most addicts and criminals don't put money aside for the inevitable arrest, despite my suggesting this to them! It's an impulse control thing. You will need to put money aside for his inevitable absence.

The good news here is that are support groups for families of incarcerated folks, such as Prison Family Alliance or Prison Fellowship that can offer guidance, resources, support groups and advice. There are millions of families across the country impacted by our broken criminal justice system, and loving a repeat offender can be hard. I encourage you to use these types of groups, because when people do not have a person with a criminal history in their lives, they can be on the "judgy" side, which is the last thing you need.

Chapter Five
He Has a Personality Disorder

As I mentioned, some untreated mental health issues are easier to manage or tolerate than others. The hardest category, in some ways, is the man who is borderline, narcissistic, or anti-social, or has obsessive compulsive personality disorder, etc. What all personality disorders have in common is **the inability to see another person's point of view. They honestly do NOT see their part of the problem**. He is perpetually victimized or put upon, and it is always your fault. There is absolutely no way to consistently "get it right," so you will live on eggshells, waiting for the next "issue" or confrontation about something you did that made him uncomfortable or disappointed.

I am thinking here about a woman I saw married to an obsessive version of this who would follow her, show up at her friend's house to try and "catch" her lying about her whereabouts, sure she was "seeing" someone else. He would berate her for hours over what he thought she might be planning if she even thought about a vacation with her girlfriends that did not include their men.

I am thinking about a man who suggested his wife start her own business and then he began to sabotage her attempts to work by complaining about her unavailability! He would then berate her for not bringing in enough income to justify her business.

I am thinking about a couple I saw twice only because it was so obvious that he had complete contempt for his wife and brought her to therapy to convince her that she was so disgusting, he would be right to throw her out of the house and try to get custody of their child.

Or another man who was so enraged when his wife left him after years of verbal abuse that he made her life a living hell by taking her to court over, and over, and over again simply to harass her and force her to pay attention to him.

What makes women choose these men? I can tell you that men like this have a tendency to enter and commit very quickly and extravagantly. They may love bomb you and make sure that you think you are the only woman they have ever really loved—everyone else they have dated or married has been an unreasonable bitch. They appear confident initially and unafraid to make decisions. This can be comforting if you are feeling a little lost yourself or have been with men who have been filled with anxiety.

If you have struggled with your own indecision and did not learn to trust yourself, it can be tempting to hand yourself over to someone who seems so SURE of himself. You are hoping to relax into being taken care of—and you will be as long as you do not deviate from his program and reflect back the image of himself that HE holds. *Essentially, he has sought a mirror in his relationships, and so that will be your role.*

The hallmark here is that it is extremely unlikely he will go to counseling or get help unless externally mandated by an employer or a judge. He might come with you once or twice to couples counseling, but only to tell the counselor all the ways YOU are the problem, and then he will not continue. Interestingly, he is not playing you or harboring some secret deep insight into his own behavior that the right counselor will uncover—what you see is what there is.

I have had women bring a man like to this to therapy with the hope that I will perform this very magic trick, and it does not happen. In fact, I have said to these men, "It sounds like you feel pretty good about yourself in the relationship. You really don't see why you should do anything differently," and they agree. They really do see her unhappiness as her problem, and they are sincere about this.

I'll be honest with you. As a therapist, I do not see a happy ending here. In fact, I usually get a sinking feeling in my gut when I see this, especially in a couple, because she is usually desperate to make this impossible partnership work and has already tried so many paths to improve the situation.

Here is what I have learned:

If you want to stay with this type of man, **you will need to create an outside life that can sustain you and provide a buffer in the face of the conflict and struggle.** Work a lot, volunteer a lot with your kid's activities, have lots of hobbies—this person will not be a steady source of support and will often find ways to say things that might cut your heart out. You will need to develop a callus when you are with them to withstand the emotional punishment they might dish out as you need to remind yourself, **"There is no way to get this right, so I might as well do what I need to do."** Try not to build such a large callus that you are numb—that is the risk.

I am thinking of a wonderful, very successful woman I knew who was married to a narcissist personality, and unfortunately over 20 years had developed an addiction to alcohol and chronic busyness to help manage her feelings about his constant onslaught of blame, accusations of infidelity, financial weaponry and withholding, and alienating her friends with aggressive intrusiveness. She was not going to truly move forward in her own healing living under this level of belittling and drama. However, she was able to build a solid support system and professional success, which helped shore her up and keep her going.

You will need to make a point of NOT talking about your relationship obsessively, even though you will be tempted because you will frequently be confused. Get a therapist and talk to her/him; your friendships and work relationships need to provide a respite for you. In fact, I would encourage you to develop strong compartmentalizing skills to move through your life until you decide if/when you will leave.

You can lose yourself in your attempts to try to stay ahead of the criticism. Don't try—these men are endlessly creative in their critical skills, and it is too much mental load to anticipate their every reaction. Live your life to the best of your ability KNOWING you will not get it right, but you can reach some of your own professional and personal goals anyway. Go for the promotion, learn a new skill, join a women's group. **Keeping your life small will not stop the complaining, so live your life as fully as you can to mitigate it.**

Find ways to spend time with your kids separately from their dad. They need a break from him, because he is critical of them too. When you get a chance to take them somewhere or join them in a hobby, I encourage you to do this. If you stay with him, they may not come to the house very much as adults, but you have managed to maintain your own relationship with them.

They know who their dad is and may even wonder if you will ever leave him. They may WISH you would leave him. While I encourage you to not bad-mouth their dad, **when they notice he is being unkind or harsh, it's okay to say that you notice that too.** It's important that they have their reality acknowledged, and they are not feeling gaslit.

I am going to repeat here:

When it goes south, the same mental illness that hijacked the marriage will also hijack the divorce proceedings and he will be difficult to work with in the separation negotiations if anyone files. **Divorce or separation is very stressful, so he will be symptomatic.** Plan on it and draw on the money you have set aside if he suddenly cancels the credit cards and withdraws all the money from the bank account. **And for God's sake, do NOT try mediation.** Go straight to an attorney. A person with an untreated personality disorder cannot negotiate in good faith, because the minute they have a new resentment or remember an old one, whatever was agreed upon will be fair game.

I can also promise you that every single time I have seen a woman leave a man who owns his own business, and used mediation to be nice, she was financially screwed. Not 75% of the time—100% of the time. PLEASE get an attorney. Playing nice will not serve you.

I have a harder time with good news here other than to refer you again to NAMI as I did in the mental health section for ongoing support and resources. It is possible to have a life when you can compartmentalize his impact on you, and you may have very real financial and familial reasons for continuing the situation. I have seen women do this for a variety of reasons, so I know it can be done. **Most importantly, be realistic about the unlikelihood of change, which will give you permission to structure your own life as fully as possible.**

Chapter Six

He Hates to Work

You have chosen a sweet man who is a real homebody! He likes to smoke weed, play video games, take care of the children. He takes them to school while you go off to work, and the other moms think he is delightful. And he is! He can be dear, helpful, good-natured—but he is not a provider and not always reliable. He might get a job, but something always happens. He might go on worker's comp, or get laid off, or walk off the job because it doesn't "work for him." Maybe he envisions creating an app or has fantasies of doing a start-up, with YOUR money.

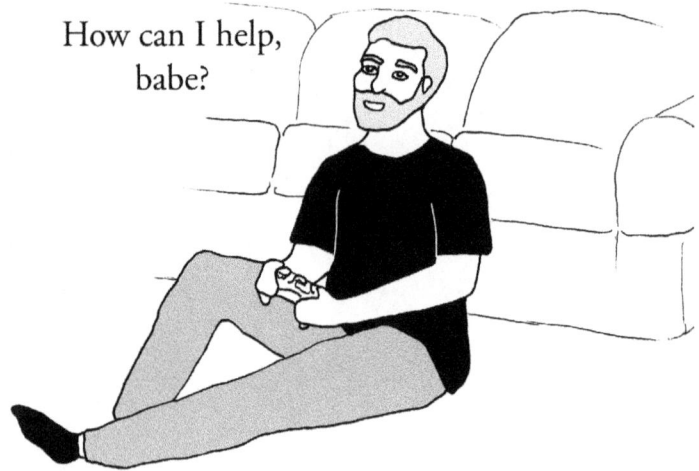

Maybe he is a garage band musician with dreams of being famous, or an artist seeing his art in the park for a few dollars. Getting a full-time job would interrupt his creative flow and sabotage his art/music career. In this case, at least you can listen to some good music or have some groovy art on the walls!

This can be a mixed bag because, on the one hand, he is the first to step in with the childcare and help around the house—**if you remind him, that is**. On the other hand, it can feel like he is another child, and you will have to really watch this. If you see him as another kid, it will kill your sex life and create enormous resentment. I think of these couples as developing a Peter Pan and Wendy dynamic, which is, unfortunately, unequal and can be toxic. A woman in this dynamic will say things to me like, "I feel like I have another kid at home." She keeps encouraging him to move forward with his professional plans, suggests resume updates, researches training institutes, even tries to make appointments for him with career coaches. **There is almost no movement in response, which leads her to feel helpless and like she is "failing" at something he has not asked her to do!**

Here is what I have learned:

Your best bet is to not lie to yourself. Don't pretend to yourself he is really creative and just needs to "find his passion or direction." Admit to yourself that you are making a trade-off. You may be choosing a sweetheart (as long as you don't push or confront him; then he is as passive-aggressive as possible), and you will need to provide the income. If you are a woman who likes a lot of control, this is the guy for you! If you do try to push him, he will complain that you are "harshing his vibe" and blame you for any negative feelings he has. On the other hand, you will get to make the major decisions that affect your life and probably control the money.

I am thinking of a wonderful couple I once knew that really struggled around this household structure. On the one hand, she appreciated how much she did not need to worry about the household while she developed her very successful career. On the other hand, she often felt left out when she came home because it was obvious the children saw him as their primary caretaker, and even seemed a little anxious when they were going to be alone with her! She proposed cutting some of her hours for more balance, which would have required him to work some. He stated that to do this he needed another degree, since he had been out of the workforce. She agreed to this, but somehow, the studies seemed to draw out and never really resulted in steady employment. Bless her, she ignored his patterns, which we so often do. **Unless people make an effort to change, their patterns will be consistent.**

It is possible that you had a really chaotic and painful childhood. Someone low maintenance and not demanding may be what your nervous system needs. **But you have to accept the arrangement and focus on what you are getting versus what he may not be providing.**

Manage your irritability when other moms tell you how lucky you are to have so much "help," and shore yourself up for the implied judgement about you because you are not as available for the school activities and play dates. There are a lot of unfair double-standards that still operate in this arena, and you will need to have other working mom friends.

No one but you will ever see the nastier side to him, which will make it even more galling when you are told how lucky you are. However, you have to weigh the WHOLE picture, and maybe overall he is still worth it.

You will need to resist pretending with your family that he is "developing an app" or some other nonsense when they ask what he is "doing" all day. I know it can be hard, but you need to embrace the man you have chosen and frame it as how fortunate you are that you never need to worry about the household, so you are free to grow professionally. You can even travel more easily.

Mostly, you will need to work through your own gender role stereotypes to be at peace with the man you have chosen, and then be able to enjoy the lifestyle you are creating. I can admit that my lifetime fantasy is to find a man who will take care of me the way my mom took care of my dad. I would love an old-fashioned wife who also happens to be sexually attractive to me, so it would be a male. All I would have to do is work and create art. Personally, I would be in heaven.

Finally, if you do decide to leave him, EXPECT to pay spousal and child support for a significant period of time. He will be entitled to an amount that allows him to retain his lifestyle, and it might be up to at least half the length of the marriage. If you are living together and not married, **get out before the ten-year mark,** because it then becomes your legal obligation to take care of him. Some women calculate it is cheaper to stay.

The good news here is that you will be in charge of how reactive you are to him. He will rarely provoke you on purpose, unlike some of the other men I discuss. **His provocation will mostly be in what he does not do, and ways he doesn't meet YOUR expectations of him**. He does want peace, especially with you. So, you can choose to relax into having a partner without professional or personal ambition as an asset, or you can be judgy and dissatisfied about it. He is who he was when you chose him, and most likely you chose him because he was flexible in a way you struggle to be. Maybe you can learn something from him!

Chapter Seven

He Is a User

This guy is a cousin to the guy who doesn't like to work, only less sweet and not as helpful. He has little to no tolerance for confrontation or questions, so will threaten to leave or throw a tantrum. Not passive aggressive—aggressive—and will feel self-righteously violated by YOUR questions.

This guy is one of the harder choices for me to understand, honestly, because he provides so little to her that it can be confusing. However, I have certainly seen lots of versions of this.

For example, the serial entrepreneur who is always nursing a new start-up idea disappears into his study for hours and days working on his idea. I saw a man like this cost his wife the $300,000 her parents had left her. Yet if she suggested that they reconsider the plan and think about more traditional employment, he punished her verbally or emotionally for not believing in him.

Or the man collecting unemployment or workers' comp who never offers to share in the household expenses. His money is HIS money. Your money is HIS money. If he does get "guilted" into paying for something for the children, his whining and resentment will diminish the victory. **Frankly, he doesn't see taking care of the family as his responsibility.** After all, YOU insisted on having them! If you DO leave him and enter another relationship, he will see the children as the new man's responsibility and not his own.

There is the version who has a trade, like a machine shop or carpentry shop, who leaves for work every day and is gone for hours and hours with no income stream. You are never invited to the shop, and you do not really know what is happening there. There is the screen writer or novelist who works hours and hours and yet never publishes. They are so "busy" on their projects, they are not available to help around the house and quickly get resentful when asked for help.

I am thinking about a woman who had been negotiating for over ten years for her husband to stop pursuing his musical career the way he was developing it because they had a child with a lot of expensive care needs, and she was working two jobs to try and make ends meet. She frequently lost sleep, had anxiety attacks, and yet he simply did not see her distress as motivating. In fact, he became rejecting and avoidant when she would raise her concerns, leaving her without help with their son. After all, who was she to ask him to sacrifice his dream?

This man is often the choice of a woman who learned to be needless and wantless in her family of origin, which may have been overstressed and chaotic. She learned to be hyper independent and may have learned that even mentioning her feelings might feel like a "trauma dump" to her caregivers and overwhelm them. So she can get very little from relationships and stretch it out for a very long time. Like a squirrel with a nut in his cheek. Some of us are very hardy squirrels.

If this is you, it may take you a long time to even recognize how little you are getting in the relationship even though others can clearly see it, because you hold on to that one time he DID come through for you.

Here is what I have learned:

In some ways, this is a fairly easy one, because you will quickly see that any financial stability will be up to you. Household maintenance and childcare will be up to you. This gives you freedom to hire a housecleaner once or twice a month if you have the resources, make childcare arrangements that are convenient to YOU, and make most of the major decisions, even though he will insist he is an equal partner. I KNOW you want to give him his dignity and go along with the fantasy that he is an equal contributor. **But if you override your judgment to have "peace," you lay the groundwork for painful resentment**. At the end of the day, his only tool is emotional blackmail, not financial planning. I KNOW your heart hurts when he threatens to leave you, and it can be tempting to give way to prevent this. I promise giving way will not prevent him from leaving, just delay it. If/when he leaves, it will be for his reasons and have very little to do with you. What you did or did not do will not matter, regardless of what he tells you.

To stave off resentment, you need to lower your expectations—in fact jettison them. If he shows up or follows through, take it as a win or delightful surprise. Plan on making the household work without him. You have mad squirrel skills, so you are probably doing this already.

Avoid nagging, blaming, raging as much as possible. Truthfully, he doesn't hear you, but YOU do, and **if you aren't careful, you will no longer recognize the woman you used to be**. To stay, you need to have a sense of humor and lots and lots of friends and personal goals and ambitions. You may not be able to reach some of them now because you are juggling everything, but eventually there will be time.

He will be a poor role model for work ethic, so know that **your children will be watching you and people you bring into their lives to learn the connection between work and money**. You will need to be explicit with this, like having a chores plan or discussing your own financial savings and decision-making, to make this real for them. If their dad contributes his philosophy, it will be along the lines of "spending money to make money" or some wish-based plan without actual steps to achieve it.

If your parents set up a college fund for your children, do not put your husband's name on the accounts. If necessary, have your parents retain the oversight of the accounts. On more than one occasion, I have seen a user guy "dip into" the college accounts to support his latest business and never replenish it. When the time comes, the money could be gone, and there will not be the same options for their education.

If your parents want to give you cash, have them pay for something your household needs like a kitchen remodel or a downpayment on a car. **This keeps the money from being fluid or accessible.**

You may want to create a trust for the children to directly inherit your assets, including taking out a life insurance plan with them as beneficiaries. **Name someone you trust as the executor to create a buffer between your man and the money.** If you do not do this, he will automatically get all your assets if you are married, and your children will not receive what you would want them to have.

There may come a time when he meets someone else who "recognizes" how fabulous he is and leaves to leech off of her. He will not provide spousal or child support—will have to be ordered to work by a judge—so plan ahead for this. **Please do not tell yourself that "when it comes down to it," he will finally show up. He will not.**

Do not believe him when he tells you he is about to get a big break, big contract, or big investor. It is not likely, because he doesn't actually work that hard. If it does happen, well, great! But I would hear it in the category of "that would be nice." Don't financially plan on it. Think of it like winning the lotto. Even if he does win this contract, he will be reluctant to share it with you because he "did all the work," so he may not even tell you the truth about the amount he is receiving.

Please try to resist investing in his "business." You will rack up extensive credit card debt, second and third mortgages, a decreased standard of living, or IRS debt. I know this will be hard because he will frame it as loving and believing in him. Offer to help in non-financial ways, like time and sweat equity, if you must.

I am thinking about the man I once knew on unemployment getting his rent paid by his parents in their 80s because they didn't KNOW he had money. He felt they owed it to him anyway, a down-payment on his inheritance, I guess. His sisters did not know the parents were doing this. Neither did his girlfriend.

I remember when I was with a man like this once, and how my gut felt when I realized that he was getting money from his elderly mother with a heart condition to support his "business." He honestly had no problem with this! I knew I was giving him money for payroll, and his wife was probably giving him money ... but Mom?

Mostly, though, I just tried not to think about this part of him and focused on the things I did enjoy about him and told myself that at some point we would be in a position to repay her. **I tried not to see it as his character but as a result of circumstances.** (I KNOW some of you reading this can relate!)

However, I was lying to myself, of course. **Don't lie to yourself.** KNOW that like the guy who doesn't work, you will need to pay spousal and child support if you leave him, and **this man will DEFINITELY fight attempts to force him to get a job** or make a living at the job he is already pretending to have. He will be nasty, so **for God's sake, do NOT try mediation**. Go straight to an attorney. He will have to be forced to move forward, and playing nice will not work. There is nothing in it for him to leave you financially, so he will drag his feet.

The good news, at least to people who love you, is that it is highly likely he will leave or force you to leave at some point, and you will need to see this as the rescue from the universe it is. As a highly loyal person, you will be appalled at how much he is willing to take from you, and you may try to placate and play nice because it is how you survived all these years. The good news is that God made attorneys for women like you, and the first thing you can do is make his attorney speak only to your attorney, and you can create a buffer between you that will allow your nervous system to start to calm down.

You can settle the relationship with a lump sum, not monthly payments, so you can be done with him and not have monthly engagements. You cannot haggle over stuff, like the TV, and walk away with your life and dignity intact. After all, YOU have a work ethic, so odds are on your side! Mostly, you must be the bad guy in his story, which you will be no matter what you do. Get support to learn to live with an unfair and untrue description of you that will be mostly built on projection, and move on. **This is not a "let's be friends" situation! Or a "California divorce," where everyone still does every holiday together. Cut and run.**

Chapter Eight

He Comes and Goes

My life has been littered with these guys! It's like loving a feral cat. I have to be honest; I am sure it is a reflection of my own ambivalence about availability. Often, these men may appear to be really "into you" initially and may even say they are falling in love with you. You have probably even seen the term "love bombing" on Tik-Tok.

The actual pattern is to say he is coming over and something always comes up; he never quite makes it. He will text in spurts. Sometimes you might have a really lengthy heart-felt exchange, and then nothing—for days. Objectively, he could not possibly be that "into" you because he never seems to actually *see* you. You are clearly not his priority, and for all you know, he might be married!

I am thinking about a woman I knew who would wait for months, even a year, to hear from the man she wanted to marry. He had ended their engagement through text, twice, but the dress was still in her closet. It was just a matter of time, right?

I am thinking of another woman who started seeing a guy who took three years to show her where he lived. He kept saying they were going to go away for the weekend—but the schedule never seemed to clear.

I once had a crush on my accountant who I saw once a year, who every time I saw him would say he was going to call me, and we would go to dinner. Five years ... no dinner.

When they do show up, it might be after you have given up, and it will look like this: "Hi." No explanation will be given, no mention of their absence, and sex will probably come up fairly quickly in the conversation. However, these guys are so feral they may even blow off a booty call date made earlier in the day—something came up! Something will always come up.

It is highly unlikely that you will need much financial protection here, because it would be rare for them to spend money on you or to ask for money. The injury here is more primitive.

It is cruel to ask someone to love you and then disappear.

One of the reasons some of us avoid love is because at some level we know **when you allow someone to love you, there is a responsibility to them that occurs. Love is a behavior, not a feeling.** So, if I say love you, it means I need to show up and participate in your life unless the relationship ends. There is an obligation to it, and there is a reward to it. Some of us did not grow up understanding this exchange. We loved without receiving the love we needed in return, so we don't experience love as a mutual exchange. It goes in only one direction. We understand the obligation, but did not experience the reward. Our inner child is hoping there is one, so we keep trying, but we pick other people who don't understand it either.

Fortunately, you can change YOUR part of this pattern, so you can learn what mutuality means, even if he never does.

Here is what I have learned:

You will never know why he does this. Do not spend thousands of dollars in therapy discussing "why" he is not responding. If you want to spend that kind of money, find out why you keep choosing him! Normally, it is because something else came up; relationships and commitment are not his priorities. It isn't personal, even though it can feel dismissive and hurtful. He might have wanted to see you when he texted, but that was hours ago!

If I were to guess, he might have an avoidant attachment style, so when he starts to have strong feelings, he gets flooded and down regulates (shoves those feelings under) until he stops having them. But then he eventually gets lonely, the feelings pop up, and he sends the "Hi" text.

It is also more fruitful for you to look at your own attachment patterns, and why you would rather get ghosted than choose someone who shows up. This is going to be the best bang for your buck! I heard a therapist say once, "You will get the intimacy you can tolerate."

There are many YouTube videos and books written trying to get insight into his pattern and yours, but I can tell you something one of my instructors told us: "**Understanding is over-rated.**" In other words, **it is the behavior that matters.** He is not going to be there with you unless he has his own reason, and then he will be gone again for his own reason. Sadly, it has nothing to do with you.

However, if you want to try and make this work, use it as a laboratory to try new behavior yourself. If you are usually afraid to be honest, this is a good guy to practice with. He comes and goes for reasons that have nothing to do with you, so give it a shot!

If you have a hard time expressing your feelings, you can practice with him, as long as you have zero expectation it will make any difference in HIS behavior. You may benefit from the practice of being honest about how you feel, even if it goes into the void he inhabits.

I was so proud of myself when I once wrote after yet another "no show,"

"_____, you have been disrespectful and hurtful to me, and I deserve better. I am not the right person for you. I wish you well."

Now, I did not use "I messages," but I actually wrote "I deserve better," and I meant it. **This was a transformative moment for me, even if it made no difference at all to him.**

After you have tried your new skills on him, consider trying to date people who ARE available. He will never know the difference, so you don't need to worry about hurting his feelings. **Please have a life while you are waiting—do not change your schedule or plans for him** because 80% of the time he will not show, or only stay a few minutes.

If he's a good booty call, I guess you could keep him as a back-up when you are in a dry spell, and he happens to show up at the right time. Just remember that it means nothing other than the immediate sexual experience, and he may or may not ever be back.

Remember that you need to invest your heart elsewhere, even if you get an occasional orgasm, if you want this guy. This relationship will never move forward.

Again, the good news is that you can go to counseling and shift this pattern. This is a learned pattern on your part, and not happening because you are fundamentally unlovable, even though that may be your interpretation. HIS behavior has nothing to do with you, and you are lovable. Some part of you knows this because you are reading this book, and your inner child has some hope that she will eventually be seen and heard accurately and be a source of joy to someone as a result!

Chapter Nine

He Is Emotionally Immature

This guy does not have a diagnosable mental health condition, though because he is moody, he might use substances leading to developing an addiction. This is the man who had early life trauma he has not addressed, and will not address, and so tends to take things personally and has poor coping skills. When under stress, he defaults to childhood coping skills like stonewalling, leaving, violence, emotional meltdowns, and more. **Think of him as "drama," because he cannot manage himself.**

There are women who come from a volatile childhood themselves with mad skills for withstanding this level of drama and may even be bored without it. They often see this as "passion," and I can admit that having dated too many engineers, a little drama can be a welcome change! In technical terms, some of us may form bonds with people who traumatize us because of our early experience, so we have our own patterns in reaction to their volatility that are as familiar to us as breathing. **They are patterns, not character, so they can change!**

It is very possible that when he is not losing his shit, he is a good companion and good with the kids. He might be smart, articulate, professional successful, a good provider. When it's good, it is very good! He may have a lot of strengths, which is why you stay. However, he will periodically be volatile, and you may not always know the trigger, so be prepared.

This reminds me of a fabulous woman I know who has spent the last 15 years with a man who periodically announces the relationship isn't working for him, citing some bogus past offense she committed towards him, and then leaves for a week. It is usually preceded by stress or conflicts at work, and he takes it out on her. It is an incredibly hurtful, and predictable, pattern. Each time, she believes he is really going to go, when it is obvious to an outsider he is just being a jackass. It takes her weeks to get past her anxiety and pain, when he seems to move past it pretty quickly and acts like nothing happened.

Or a woman married to a man who will get a resentment about her behavior that eats away at him, and they fight until they find a solution. However, even when the solution has been found, he still suggests he needs "space" because he can't forgive her. She feels punished, because she IS being emotionally punished.

Or being with a man who interprets every disappointment as proof that he doesn't matter or you don't love him, which is followed by several hours of heavy and emotional conversation to reassure him. It is exhausting.

If you are drawn to these types of men, it is possible you have some impressive skills for addressing other people's anxiety—you see anxiety as a "crisis" requiring immediate intervention. Maybe as a kid, if a volatile adult was not soothed, chaos and even violence might break out. So you are a human tuning fork for anxiety and are quick to move into action.

Here is what I have learned:

If you love one of these men, you will need to learn quickly to not take their reactivity personally. These guys often lose proportion and may overreact or underreact, neither of which may have to do with the actual situation. You will need to develop some strong emotional regulation skills of your own to not be pulled into his anxiety and chaos.

This means you will have to strengthen your internal observer to "observe" their behavior and take a little time to respond, even if you have to count to ten or walk away and use the bathroom to breathe. Your instinct will be to jump in with him, and then you are both drowning. Yes, he will interpret your observational stance as "not caring," but YOU know that your ability to manage your own reactivity can reduce the amount of time and energy this latest "crisis" will take to resolve. Over time, the drama can reduce, although will not completely disappear.

Unfortunately, one of his coping skills might be to "punish" you with financial control, and he can be either generous or withholding. If he is generous with jewelry, borrow from the "married guy" advice and keep it handy or in your safety deposit box to sell later if you need to. **I would encourage you to PLAN for a withholding possibility by applying the earlier advice to have your own income stream, have your own bank account, develop your own credit, and have money set aside for this.**

You can also get some cash every time you buy groceries and stash the cash in your own account to have access to some money if you need it. Our grandmothers and great grandmothers knew to do this—it might save your bacon. In fact, my grandmother always had a twenty in her bra "just in case."

If he's volatile, he may throw and break things; hopefully not you, though that is a sad possibility. **More likely he will resort to intimidation strategies like having a tantrum, so you may need to occasionally get walls or doors repaired or replace broken objects.** Have a good handyman on speed dial.

In fact, his tantrums may spill over to the neighbors, extended family, or co-workers, which can make maintaining relationships and even a job challenging for him. **Do not apologize for him; just maintain your OWN relationships separately.** It is possible that his volatility may make it unwise to take him along in some situations, like your child's soccer tournament, because he cannot handle himself. Certainly, apply the earlier financial advice to prepare for potential unemployment because of conflict on the job.

You may not always know what he is upset about, because it probably isn't about you. These men are carrying some old wounds, and they can get unexpectedly triggered by even minor slights and have very poor resilience. So they look outside of themselves for an explanation for their emotional discomfort, and you or "the burdens of the family" may become that explanation. Do your best to resist playing "therapist" when they are having a meltdown. **You do not want to become his "binky" every time he has a large feeling.** It will burn you out and may lead you to lose respect for him. You can be kind, but don't take over as "the good mom." Instead, use your own emotional regulation skills, and if he is a sulker, just let him sulk in another room while you carry on the household structure.

When he is in a more stable period, following a "losing his shit" period, he might agree to couples counseling. I strongly recommend this, as you both can develop better communication skills and at least dial down some of the drama, if not all of it. I see a lot of these couples, and I know having therapy support can be helpful. Very frequently these men are shame-based, and we can SEE the child they were who was not seen and heard, and our hearts can go out to them. It's one of the reasons we stay. There can be a sweetness under there that pops out from time to time that is also part of their inner child.

A huge step forward will be when YOU learn not to react to his overwhelm and stay centered in yourself. It will pass, it always does, and you matching his level of chaos only draws out the incident. It will also force him to work on his own issues if you step away from playing therapist and refer him to one instead.

If he is violent, though, couples counseling is dangerous, and you may need more imminent support like having a safety plan. Your safety plan should include:

- a list of local shelters or safe friends in case you need to flee with little notice;
- a packed bag with some clothes, your passport, and some money;
- a bag for your children with their medicine, clothes, a few toys.

Stash the bags at a safe person's house so you can get in the car and run and won't have to lose time gathering your belongings. **I hope you will never need this plan, but if you do, do not hesitate. RUN.**

If you call 911, it is highly likely that at least one of you will be arrested, and hopefully it will be him. You need to prepare for his quick release because that will be a more dangerous time. **Again, you might have at least 24 hours** to more methodically pack and move, or change the locks, or file a restraining order—whatever you need to do. Just act quickly because it is possible he will be released on his own recognizance and then head home pissed off and resentful over what YOU have done to him.

You might reconcile at some point, but always, always, have a safety plan unless he does something dramatic to change.

This reminds me—**domestic violence classes for 52 weeks costs money. He has to pay every session. Same thing for "Parenting without Violence." Supervised visitation also costs money—up to $100 per session.** If he is charged with domestic violence, you will also have legal fees and court costs.

Again, I am not judging, and women stay with volatile men for many, many reasons. I just want you to be safe and financially prepared if this is your choice.

The good news is these patterns can change! I have seen individuals and couples learn to dial down the reactivity though counseling and sometimes mediation to stabilize the situation. They shorten their conflict periods and strengthen their repair skills. They are able to successfully co-parent and can learn empathy for each other's attachment style and patterns, so they can be of genuine comfort to each other in a more mutual way. **My caveat here is that violence patterns do not always change,** and so if the volatility continues to be dangerous, you will have to find a way to be safe.

You are most at risk of serious violence when you finally leave, so PLEASE reach out to agencies like Next Door and other women's violence prevention agencies to do the preparation you need to leave safely.

Chapter Ten

He's a Cheater

I saved the best for last in some ways. This situation is probably one of the more common ones I see, and it is universally painful. Despite the lying, the tearful remorse scenes, the cold silences of disdain we express to punish them while they grovel . . . we stay. Sometimes we tell ourselves it is for the kids; sometimes because of pride; sometimes we are too stubborn to quit. Many, many women make their peace with this situation over time. Women throughout history have done so, and there are some ways to stay sane if you decide to make it work.

I can honestly tell you that very rarely is infidelity in long-term stable relationships only about one person. Usually, it is the result of both parties who have allowed a gap to be created in their connection, and then normalized it instead of addressing it. In this case, if both people can see their role in the gap, I have seen the marriage get repaired and become stronger. It is not true that infidelity HAS to be a relationship-ender, though it often is.

In the case of serial cheating, something else is going on. There are women who prefer to remain in denial about the other relationships, and others who operate like terriers sniffing out any whiff of another person. Neither of these approaches will result in emotional sanity, and both will keep you from living your OWN life because you are too preoccupied with HIS life! You are trying to control something you do not have the power to control. As we say in recovery, you need to *surrender* your death grip on him.

Similar to the section where we choose a married man, we may stay with a man who is unfaithful because we learned to make imbalanced relationships work. We learned as kids to lower our expectations and ignore our own needs to keep the attachment, so we do not see ourselves as competent enough to make the hard decisions we would need to make. We might roll into learned helplessness when faced with a relationship threat. So we might yell and scream or ice him out, but we don't leave.

Here is what I have learned:

Don't lie to yourself about who he is. Your best path to sanity is to tell yourself the truth about who this man is, and don't let yourself get surprised and horrified when he acts out again with another person. It will not be surprising when he does it again; it is predictable.

Remember my blue bathrobe guy? He got divorced before meeting me because he had met someone ONLINE and started an affair with her. I knew this, and yet when it happened in our relationship, I felt shocked at first! I should not have been. It was predictable. No doubt he went through another depressive episode in his marriage and "treated" his depression the same way. He tried to treat it by finding another person as his mood regulator.

I should not have been shocked when the married guy dumped me for another bimbo because he was already cheating on his wife with me! Honestly, it was predictable. **So, tell yourself the truth about the relationship you have chosen.**

Remember that the cheating is not about you. I know this can be hard. We tend to think, "Maybe if I was thinner, taller, more successful, younger ... he wouldn't cheat." If he has a personality disorder, he has probably told you this. It is not true. When people are serially cheating, it is about them and not the woman they are with. Think about celebrity men you know who have cheated on their beautiful wives.

Consider calling it an open marriage, so it isn't cheating. I know this is controversial, but it is a way to make peace with the situation you have chosen. You do not have to act on this open situation unless you want to. It creates a different definition of the relationship that realistically calls it what it is.

Be clear about WHY you are staying and the pros of the relationship that outweigh the cons. He might occasionally see other women, but he may also be a good companion, good with the kids, a solid provider, nice to your parents; you have your reasons. Maybe you aren't really into sex yourself and are kind of relieved that you don't have to feel guilty about it, because he's getting his needs met.

Create some ground rules you can live with. For example, he can't date your sister. He has to come home every night. He can't use your joint account to buy her presents or take her to YOUR favorite restaurant. He can't see her publicly and embarrass you—keep it on the down-low. Make sure he uses a condom. The two of you can have an honest conversation about what you can live with. Again, **NO PRETENDING.**

Take care of your sexual and physical health. Is he going to strip clubs but not having sex? Is it porn where he masturbates? Or is he seeing prostitutes and hooking up randomly? You need to know this because you need to make sexual decisions yourself to stay safe. If you choose to continue your sexual relationship with him, use protection as long as he is acting out this pattern. You can also request that he get tested for sexually transmitted diseases like HIV and Hep-C. I know it is unpleasant to think of, but so are genital warts and chlamydia.

Let go of what others would say. At the end of the day, every marriage is its own universe. Saying "I would never put up with that" is easy for someone who has never been faced with it. Frankly, your relationship is none of anyone's business.

Have your own fulfilling life outside of marriage so that you can **compartmentalize this aspect**. You are a whole person with a lot of different facets. Your relationship and HIS behavior is only one facet. Do not let it get outsized and lose its proportion. You are more than your relationship.

The good news here is that you are not alone, and there is a powerful support group, S-Anon, which is a Twelve-Step group for family and friends of sex addicts, much like Al-Anon is for Alcoholics. You can learn to use tools to help yourself remain emotionally stable in the face of his behaviors and can learn to drop the terrier behavior that is making you ill. You can share your story and get encouragement from the success of other people who are managing this situation well.

There are also residential and outpatient treatment centers for sex addicts if/when he decides to address his pattern and change. In the meantime, you can take care of you.

Conclusion

When I look back over the years and see the roll call of BAD TASTE choices I, and women like me, have made, what has saved us over and over again is structuring our lives to function with or without him. We may have lived with him, but he moved into OUR house, so when it ended, he moved out of OUR house. We had separate finances. We kept our basic infrastructure solid so the chaos would not be permanent. I know this is not romantic, but it is necessary and practical.

By the way, I am not anti-marriage and have seen many wonderful, loving partnerships over the years. So if you have GOOD TASTE, go for it!

Can you change this pattern? Again, I am a therapist and have spent 40 years watching people take emotional and relational risks and **absolutely** change this trajectory. There are many books and resources to help you make these changes. There are therapy approaches ranging from Cognitive Behavioral Therapy (CBT) to Internal Family Systems (IFS) to guide you. I have shifted this pattern myself, though I will not pretend it does not take years to do. There is no quick fix to early attachment disruption, but there is success along the way until we actually come to believe we ARE lovable and develop an inner parent that will choose in our best interests.

The truth is, THEY see the package we offer more clearly than we do. THEY see our nice living environment, strong work ethic, willingness to work as a team, our sense of humor, how kind we can be—**we** are the ones who don't see it. It takes work for us to see ourselves more clearly, and it can get better and better. When I think about my own process, I can see where my inner child now says, "I want to play with him!" and my inner adult says, "I know honey, but he can't have a play date with you. I'm sorry." I don't protest (ruminate) as much or as long. I surrender to the part of me that is protective more easily.

But if you can honestly look at your history and know that you have a radar for the most inappropriate choice in the room, even if you are working on it, protect your assets if you are about to again step into the void. As my friends could tell you, if my eyes were lighting up about a guy, they already knew he was most likely a no-hoper!

This little book is written for people who are working on this pattern, more resigned to their pattern, maybe old enough to know what they are more likely to do, or know that the only way it would be different is divine intervention. After all, as the saying goes, "The heart wants what it wants!" Please don't hesitate to check out the resources I have mentioned. You are not alone with your patterns, if you choose to change them.

I am glad my home girl encouraged me to write my thoughts down because these are conversations I have had over the years with so many women. I love us, and I know how hard we try to make what can seem like insurmountable relationships work. We are so hardy, resilient, clever. Remember that regardless of what HE does, you are a separate and fabulous woman, and he should be damn grateful you will put up with him! None of these guys are worthy to carry our purse, and yet we love them anyway. Lucky them!

**Quizzes to Consider if You
are on a Journey to Shift Your Patterns**

**Could start and interesting chat
with your therapist. . . . .**

What Is My Attachment Style?

The first step toward applying attachment theory to *your* life is to get to know yourself and those around you from an attachment perspective. In the next chapter, we'll walk you through the process of determining your partner or prospective partner's attachment style based on various clues. But let's begin by assessing the person you know best—yourself.

Which Attachment Style Am I?

Following is a questionnaire designed to measure your attachment style—the way you relate to others in the context of intimate relationships. This questionnaire is based on the Experience in Close Relationship (ECR) questionnaire. The ECR was first published in 1998 by Kelly Brennan, Catherine Clark, and Phillip Shaver, the same Shaver who published the original "love quiz" with Cindy Hazan. The ECR allowed for specific short questions that targeted particular aspects of adult attachment based on two main categories: anxiety in the relationship and avoidance. Later, Chris Fraley from the University of Illinois, together with Niels Waller and Kelly Brennan, revised the questionnaire to create the ECR-R. We present a modified version that we think works best in everyday life.

Attachment styles are stable but plastic. Knowing your specific attachment profile will help you understand yourself better and guide you in your interactions with others. Ideally this will result in more happiness in your relationships. (For a fully validated adult attachment questionnaire, you can log on to Dr. Chris Fraley's website at: http://www.web-research-design.net/cgi-bin/crq/crq.pl.)

Check the small box next to each statement that is TRUE for you.
(If the answer is untrue, *don't* mark the item at all.)

	TRUE		
	A	B	C
I often worry that my partner will stop loving me.	☐		
I find it easy to be affectionate with my partner.		☐	
I fear that once someone gets to know the real me, s/he won't like who I am.	☐		

I find that I bounce back quickly after a breakup. It's weird how I can just put someone out of my mind.			☐
When I'm not involved in a relationship, I feel somewhat anxious and incomplete.	☐		
I find it difficult to emotionally support my partner when s/he is feeling down.			☐
When my partner is away, I'm afraid that s/he might become interested in someone else.	☐		

	TRUE		
	A	B	C
I feel comfortable depending on romantic partners.		☐	
My independence is more important to me than my relationships.			☐
I prefer not to share my innermost feelings with my partner.			☐
When I show my partner how I feel, I'm afraid s/he will not feel the same about me.	☐		
I am generally satisfied with my romantic relationships.		☐	
I don't feel the need to act out much in my romantic relationships.		☐	
I think about my relationships a lot.	☐		
I find it difficult to depend on romantic partners.			☐
I tend to get very quickly attached to a romantic partner.	☐		
I have little difficulty expressing my needs and wants to my partner.		☐	
I sometimes feel angry or annoyed with my partner without knowing why.			☐
I am very sensitive to my partner's moods.	☐		
I believe most people are essentially honest and dependable.		☐	

I prefer casual sex with uncommitted partners to intimate sex with one person.			☐
I'm comfortable sharing my personal thoughts and feelings with my partner.		☐	

	TRUE		
	A	**B**	**C**
I worry that if my partner leaves me I might never find someone else.	☐		
It makes me nervous when my partner gets too close.			☐
During a conflict, I tend to impulsively do or say things I later regret, rather than be able to reason about things.	☐		
An argument with my partner doesn't usually cause me to question our entire relationship.		☐	
My partners often want me to be more intimate than I feel comfortable being.			☐
I worry that I'm not attractive enough.	☐		
Sometimes people see me as boring because I create little drama in relationships.		☐	
I miss my partner when we're apart, but then when we're together I feel the need to escape.			☐
When I disagree with someone, I feel comfortable expressing my opinions.		☐	
I hate feeling that other people depend on me.			☐
If I notice that someone I'm interested in is checking out other people, I don't let it faze me. I might feel a pang of jealousy, but it's fleeting.		☐	
If I notice that someone I'm interested in is checking out other people, I feel relieved—it means s/he's not looking to make things exclusive.			☐
If I notice that someone I'm interested in is checking out other people, it makes me feel depressed.	☐		
If someone I've been dating begins to act cold and distant, I may wonder what's happened, but I'll know it's probably not about me.		☐	

	TRUE		
	A	B	C
If someone I've been dating begins to act cold and distant, I'll probably be indifferent; I might even be relieved.			☐
If someone I've been dating begins to act cold and distant, I'll worry that I've done something wrong.	☐		
If my partner was to break up with me, I'd try my best to show her/him what s/he is missing (a little jealousy can't hurt).	☐		
If someone I've been dating for several months tells me s/he wants to stop seeing me, I'd feel hurt at first, but I'd get over it.		☐	
Sometimes when I get what I want in a relationship, I'm not sure what I want anymore.			☐
I won't have much of a problem staying in touch with my ex (strictly platonic) — after all, we have a lot in common.		☐	

*Adapted from Fraley, Waller, and Brennan's (2000) ECR-R Questionnaire.

Add up all your checked boxes in column A: _____

Add up all your checked boxes in column B: _____

Add up all your checked boxes in column C: _____

Scoring Key

The more statements that you check in a category, the more you will display characteristics of the corresponding attachment style. Category A represents the *anxious attachment* style, Category B represents the *secure* attachment style, and Category C represents the *avoidant* attachment style.

Anxious: You love to be very close to your romantic partners and have the capacity for great intimacy. You often fear, however, that your partner does not wish to be as close as you would like him/her to be. Relationships tend to consume a large part of your emotional energy.

You tend to be very sensitive to small fluctuations in your partner's moods and actions, and although your senses are often accurate, you take your partner's behaviors too personally. You experience a lot of negative emotions within the relationship and get easily upset. As a result, you tend to act out and say things you later regret. If the other person provides a lot of security and reassurance, however, you are able to shed much of your preoccupation and feel contented.

Secure: Being warm and loving in a relationship comes naturally to you. You enjoy being intimate without becoming overly worried about your relationships. You take things in stride when it comes to romance and don't get easily upset over relationship matters. You effectively communicate your needs and feelings to your partner and are strong at reading your partner's emotional cues and responding to them. You share your successes and problems with your mate, and are able to be there for him or her in times of need.

Avoidant: It is very important for you to maintain your independence and self-sufficiency and you often prefer autonomy to intimate relationships. Even though you do want to be close to others, you feel uncomfortable with too much closeness and tend to keep your partner at arm's length. You don't spend much time worrying about your romantic relationships or about being rejected. You tend not to open up to your partners and they often complain that you are emotionally distant. In relationships, you are often on high alert for any signs of control or impingement on your territory by your partner.

Responses to Stressful Experiences Scale

The following statements describe how some individuals may think, feel, or act during and after the most stressful events in life. Please indicate how well each of these statements describes you during and after life's most stressful events.

4	3	2	1	0
Exactly Like Me				Not at All Like Me

During and after life's most stressful events, I tend to …

1. …take action to fix things.
2. …not give up trying to solve problems I think I can solve.
3. …find a way to do what's necessary to carry on.
4. …pray or meditate.
5. …face my fears.
6. …find opportunity for growth.
7. …calm and comfort myself.
8. …try to "recharge" myself before I have to face the next challenge.
9. …see it as a challenge that will make me better.
10. …look at the problem in a number of ways.
11. …look for creative solutions to the problem.
12. …put things in perspective and realize I will have times of joy and times of sadness.
13. …be good at determining which situations *are* changeable and which *are not*.
14. …find meaning from the experience.
15. …find strength in the meaning, purpose, or mission of my life.
16. …know I will bounce back.
17. …expect that I can handle it.
18. …learn important and useful life lessons.
19. …understand that bad things can happen to anyone, not just me.
20. …lean on my faith in God or a higher power.

21. ...draw upon lessons learned from failures and past mistakes.
22. ...practice ways to handle it better next time.

Scoring and Algorithm

> **Note:** For each assessment, there is a scoring algorithm leading to one of three acuity ranges: Low, Moderate, or High
> The items are scored 0-4 as described below.

Total score is sum of all 22 items, possible range 0 – 88.

Algorithm

Total = 71 – 88   High Resilience

Total = 50 – 70   Moderate Resilience

Total =   0 – 49   Low Resilience

Mary Crocker Cook

Contact Information

www.badtasteinmen.com

For more information about my counseling services or presentation topics visit www.marycrockercook.com

Mary Crocker Cook
1710 Hamilton Ave. #8
San Jose, CA 95125.

Phone: (408) 448-0333

Email: marycook@connectionscounselingassociates.com

Notes

www.ingramcontent.com/pod-product-compliance
Lightning Source LLC
Chambersburg PA
CBHW071333190426
43193CB00041B/1761